# Dark Age Dorset

Robert Westw
robert.westwood3@btinte

First published in 200
*Inspiring Places Publishing*
2 Down Lodge Close
Alderholt
Fordingbridge
Hampshire
SP63JA

ISBN 978-0-9552061-3-9

Printed by ACH Colour, Bournemouth

*Inspiring Places Publishing*

# Contents



Other titles by *Inspiring Places Publishing:*
Fossils and Rocks of the Jurassic Coast
Ancient Dorset
Day Tours in the East of Dorset
Smugglers' Dorset
Mysterious Places of Dorset
Alien Big Cats of Dorset

Check these out and visit the photo gallery at *www.inspiringplaces.co.uk.*

Front cover: The statue of King Alfred in the gardens of Shaftesbury Abbey. [by kind permission of Shaftesbury Abbey and Gardens]
Rear cover: St. Martin's Wareham - a Saxon church
Title page: The Silver Well, Cerne Abbas

# Introduction

The phrase "the Dark Ages" has traditionally been used by historians to describe the period after the fall of Rome in the 5th century to around AD 1000 when some sort of political stability was generally assumed to have returned to Europe. In Britain this coincides with the time from when the Roman legions left to the Norman Conquest.

The term was first coined by Petrarch in the 1330s. Petrarch was a humanist who mourned the loss of classical art and literature. Humanists believed the Roman Empire would rise again and that Latin, art and architecture would flourish once more. They included their own era as a "dark age".

Originally many people agreed with Petrarch that civilisation had indeed taken a backward step but gradually historians came to realise that many parts of western Europe carried on in an organised and civilised fashion after the Romans. Instead they used the term "Dark Ages" in a more neutral manner, linking the term to the fact that there was a relative paucity of information about this period.

With modern archaeology more and more is now known about these times. In Britain there were undoubtedly tremendous upheavals. Towns were abandoned and money ceased to be used: these are profound changes. We know something of the political crises from one or two monks who continued to write in Latin. The Anglo-Saxons have left us very good written records, notably the Anglo-Saxon Chronicles.

There is no doubt these were exciting times and the lack of information has added to their perceived glamour, leading to the emergence of powerful legends such as King Arthur. Christianity had only recently come to these islands and had to start again when the heathen Anglo-Saxons took over. Then there were the Vikings; ferocious raiders who must have struck fear into every inhabitant.

Throughout this time Dorset was in the centre of things. A flourishing, peaceful area under the Romans, on their leaving it became part of a British kingdom of the south-west where trade continued to prosper. Very soon it was on the edge of an early Saxon settlement, but enjoyed about 50 more years of peace and prosperity after the famous battle of Mount Badon [thanks to Arthur?]. Finally conquered by the Saxons it settled down again until it became the first part of the British Isles to experience a Viking raid. Thanks to Alfred the Great peace was re-established and Dorset became part of the kingdom of Wessex, enjoying something of a golden age under him and his descendants such as King Edgar.

The Vikings returned however, and Dorset plunged once more into "dark" times. Despite being once soundly beaten on Dorset soil the Viking king, Canute became king of all England and was reputedly very fond of Dorset; he died in Shaftesbury Abbey.

Our story finishes in 1086. Dorset had been conquered once again, by the Normans. In the aftermath of 1066 things might not have seemed that much different; Anglo-Saxon rural life probably went on much as before. Following rebellions in the north and south-west, however, the Normans ravaged the countryside and towns, leaving few Anglo-Saxons as landholders. In 1086 they decided to do a survey of what they now owned: it has survived to us as the Domesday Book.

*Below: The ancient village of Cerne Abbas sits beneath the enigmatic figure of its famous giant carved in the chalk hill side.*

# *Dark Age Dorset Timeline*

**AD**

**410** *Rome abandons Britain - the emperor Honorius tells Britain it must look after itself, Roman legions leave. Britain is probably ruled by petty tyrants. Dorset probably part of the kingdom of Dumnonia.*

**425** *Vortigern emerges as the most powerful ruler in Britain. He probably governs via a council of some sort.*

**437** *Ambrosius Aurelianus becomes leader of Pro-Roman faction. He is victorious against Vortigern's relative Vitalinus at a battle near Wallop in Hampshire. There is civil war and famine in Britain.*

**446** *The Britons appeal to the emperor Aetius in Rome, but he has his hands full with Attila the Hun.*

**450** *The Saxon leaders Hengest and Horsa arrive in southern England at the request of Vortigern to help fight the Picts.*

**460** *Ambrosius Aurelianus defeats Vortigern and assumes control. Years of fighting with Saxons ensues.*

**496** *Saxons defeated at battle of Mount Badon. Britons possibly led by Arthur under the command of an old Ambrosius? Period of relative peace - Dorset still part of a British kingdom.*

**519** *Saxon Kingdom of Wessex founded with Cerdic its first ruler. Around 540 Gildas writes his history, possibly in Dorset.*

**552** *King Cynric of Wessex defeats Britons at Old Sarum. Is this the beginning of the end for Dorset as part of a British kingdom? In 597 Augustine lands in Britain.*

**658** *King Cenwalh of Wessex defeats Britons of Dumnonia at Penselwood. The boundary of Wessex is set at the River Parrett in Somerset. Thus Dorset is still on the border between Wessex and the remaining British kingdoms.*

**787** *First Viking raid recorded in Portland, Dorset.*

**870** *Wessex stands alone. The rest of England is controlled by the Danes.*

**AD**

**878** *King Alfred of Wessex defeats the Danes and establishes Wessex as the most powerful Saxon kingdom.*
*Relative peace in England - the golden age of Wessex, culminating in the reign of King Edgar.*

**978** *Edgar's successor, Edward is murdered at Corfe Castle. Ethelred the Unready becomes king and Viking attacks resume.*

**1016** *The Dane Canute becomes king of England, though not before being beaten in battle by Edmund Ironside at Gillingham, Dorset.*
*When Canute's line died out Edward the Confessor restored the English line to the throne.*

**1066** *Duke William of Normandy defeats English at Hastings and becomes king. Saxon nobles are largely dispossessed and huge tracts of the country ravaged following rebellions.*

**1086** *Domesday survey undertaken.*

*Below: The Constable's Hall, Christchurch - part of the Norman castle built by Baron de Redvers after the conquest. It stands by the mill stream, used by the Saxons for several hundred years. After all these years still a typical English scene!*

# Some places of interest in Dark Age Dorset

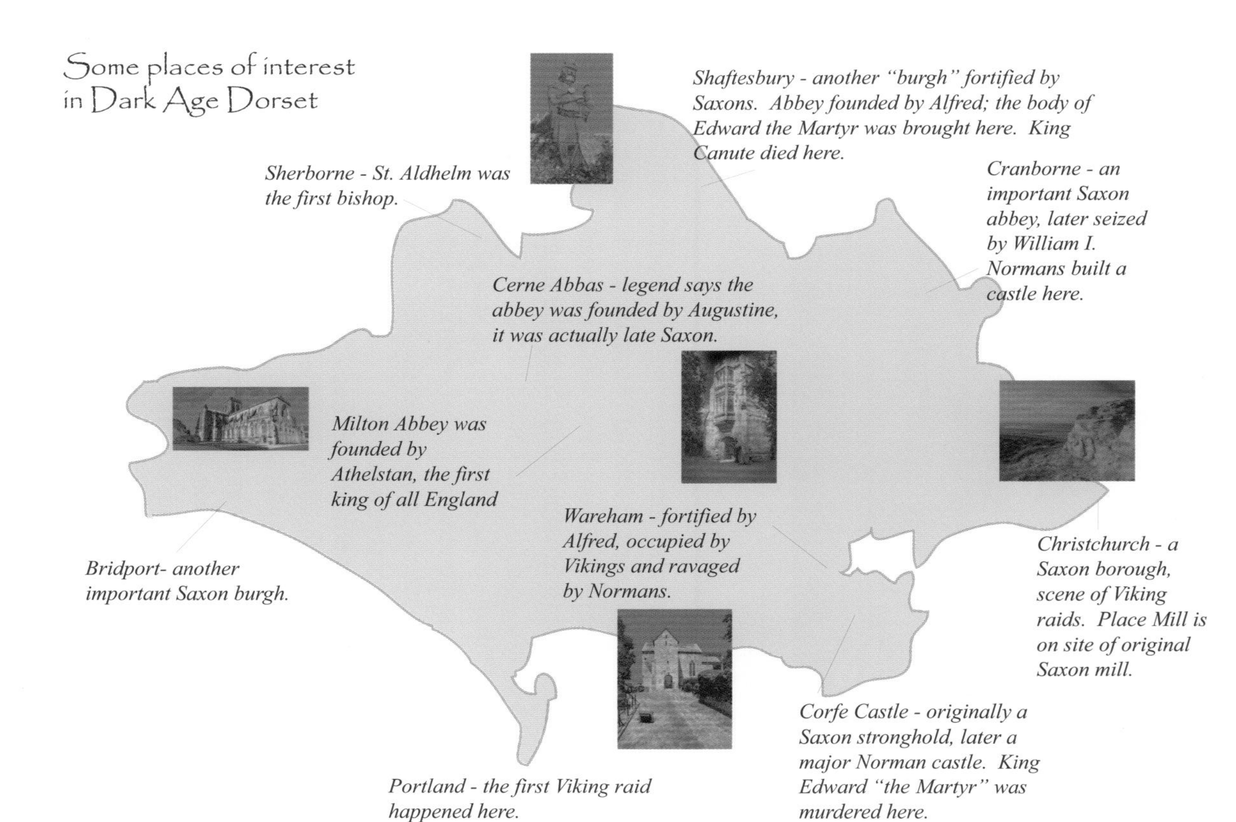

# After the Romans

*Above: Ancient Britons did not look out over these battlements at Tintagel, and certainly not King Arthur, but there was a major Dark Age settlement here in what was the kingdom of Dumnonia.*

What happened after the Roman legions departed Britain? This is a question that has interested scholars for decades. It used to be assumed that the country descended into a barbaric dark age, with a rapid disintegration of the infrastructure built up by the Romans. Evidence of re-occupation of Iron Age hillforts tended to support this, suggesting that the sophisticated urban centres were no longer safe places to live. Out of these Dark Ages came the most powerful of British legends, that of King Arthur, a heroic war leader who stemmed the tide of Saxon invaders and created a glorious but ephemeral peace.

Academic opinion has now shifted and many people believe that civilisation did continue to flourish after the Roman withdrawal. There is increasing evidence of the continued usage of sophisticated Latin and finds of luxury imported goods at places like Tintagel suggest a more coherent and cultured society than had previously been imagined, and one that had extensive links with continental Europe. There is no doubt, however, that many Roman towns were abandoned or that there were many political crises. There were many small British kingdoms at this time and it is thought Dorset was part of one of the largest, known as Dumnonia and covering what is now Cornwall, Devon, Somerset and Dorset. Famous sites such as Cadbury and Tintagel may have been important centres.

It is generally accepted that Anglo-Saxon settlement began in southern England around AD 450. The much criticised British leader Vortigern is credited with recruiting Saxon mercenaries for help against the Picts and Scots. Vortigern is an enigmatic figure. What we know of him comes from later sources. At the time he was probably the most powerful man in Britain although there is nothing to suggest he was a sort of high king of the British. He seems to have exercised his powers through and with a council of some sort. The Saxons soon began to expand from their base in the south-east and others followed them from the continent.

The Saxon leaders Cerdic and Cynric landed at Southampton Water in AD 495 and quickly established a settlement. Dorset remained untouched, however, and British resistance was co-ordinated by Ambrosius Aurelianus, under whom a great victory over the Saxons was achieved at Mons Badonicus [or Mount Badon] around AD 500. This pivotal battle, often associated with the legendary King Arthur, resulted in a period of peace and a resurgence of British culture. The great earthwork of Bokerley Dyke on the Hampshire/Dorset border dates from this time and is thought to have been constructed as a defence against the Saxons. It indicates that the British leaders were able to mobilise large numbers of workers for a cooperative effort. Ambrosius Aurelianus is another figure shrouded in mystery. He is generally accepted as an historical figure but who he actually was is still unclear. Some sources say he was descended from a Roman emperor and there are stories of his collaboration with a certain Merlin. His power base has been claimed to have been in modern Wiltshire around Amesbury, but this is far from certain. Ambrosius is the only figure mentioned by name by the monk Gildas who wrote his famous treatise "Concerning the Ruin of Britain" in the 6th century. His vitriolic prose condemns the warring British leaders apart from Ambrosius and laments the gradual conquest of Britain by the heathen invaders. It is the only contemporary, written account of the Anglo-Saxon settlement in Britain.

Some people associate the Iron Age hillfort of Badbury Rings with the Battle of Mons Badonicus and it certainly fits in with a likely attempt to expand from a base around Southampton. However, it is only one of a number of suggested locations. Wherever it happened the result was around fifty years more peace for the inhabitants of Dorset. Inevitably the Saxon advance resumed and Dorset eventually became part of the Saxon kingdom of Wessex.

## Badbury Rings

Badbury Rings can be found on the B3082 north-west of Wimborne heading towards Blandford Forum. Turn right into the large car park in the middle of the famous and beautiful avenue of beech trees, originally three hundred and sixty five of them on each side. Sadly the trees are now coming to the end of their natural life but the National Trust has planted replacements by the side of the old beeches.

Badbury is an impressive hillfort with three concentric ditches and ramparts. The interior is now heavily wooded but there are fine views from the banks. Badbury was probably a stronghold of the Durotriges tribe, like its neighbour Maiden Castle. It has never been excavated but it is likely that it was besieged and taken by the Romans during their conquest of southern Britain. A number of Bronze Age burial barrows can be seen just outside the fort, indicating it has been a place of some significance for thousands of years.

The important Roman road from Dorchester to Old Sarum runs just west of Badbury and this no doubt intensified the speculation of some that Badbury was the site of Mons Badonicus, the famous battle where Arthur defeated the Germanic invaders. As we have seen, logically and geographically this makes some sense, but many scholars favour a location around the present city of Bath. Whatever the truth, Badbury may have still been an important location in the era we are considering and it is certainly a good place for a walk and a picnic.

# King Arthur

It is a daunting task to write anything about King Arthur. Search the web or Amazon and you will find a bewildering and overwhelming number of articles and books about him. Learned scholars have written about him as have new age romantics. As Britain's foremost legendary hero this is perhaps quite appropriate. His presence has been claimed and his influence inferred in many areas, from Cornwall to the north of England and from Wales to Somerset. Even Dorset has alleged Arthurian associations.

Academic opinion seems divided about whether Arthur was a real historic figure. All are agreed that, if he was, he was some sort of military leader at the time when Britain was under threat from Anglo-Saxon invaders and settlers. He may have been a key figure in a number of battles where the Britons were victorious over the Saxons, culminating in the defining conflict, the Battle of Mount Badon or Mons Badonicus. This key, and real, victory was a temporary turning point in the struggle and resulted in around fifty years of relative peace; a mini golden age perhaps. Many people have sought to establish that there was a real person around this time named Arthur who, by his leadership and military prowess, inspired this British revival. Unfortunately the written records are tantalisingly sparse. It is well known that the monk Gildas, writing around this time, does not mention Arthur at all. Nor does Bede in his "Ecclesiastical History of the English Nation". Arthur appears in short references in "The History of the Britons" by the Welsh writer Nennius in the 8th century. Modern scholars regard Nennius as unreliable historically, but he may have had access to other sources which are no longer around. Arthur is also mentioned in ancient Welsh chronicles.

There are many sources of information for the interested reader. This is not the place to delve into the question of whether there was an historical Arthur and who he was, but it is interesting to consider where Dorset fits into this story. As Geoffrey Ashe, perhaps the country's leading Arthurian scholar, has pointed out, it is pertinent to investigate where the myth emanated from, rather than trying to find an historical figure.

As we have seen, at the time of Arthur, Dorset was probably part of a British kingdom. Saxons had established bases on its border - if anywhere was going to feel threatened by the heathen invaders it was Dorset. We have noted that a defensive earthwork was constructed or enhanced around this time, Bokerley Dyke, now on the Dorset/ Hampshire border. It seems likely that after the Romans left, Dorset had continued to enjoy a measure of peace and prosperity. This is just the sort of environment out of which stories of an heroic war leader would emerge.

Dorset's main "Arthurian site" is Badbury Rings, claimed by some to have been the scene of the Battle of Mount Badon. Sadly, there is no evidence of the Saxons being anywhere near there in the 6th century and most scholars do not favour Badbury as the site of this climactic battle. Nevertheless, we do know the Saxons were not far from here and Badbury has never been excavated. With poor heathlands to the east stretching all the way to Southampton Water, it has been argued that Badbury is a gateway to the rich agricultural lands to the west; just the path the Saxons would have chosen to take. Roy Carr, writing in "Dorset Life" argues strongly that Badbury was the site, citing the fact that several mutilated bodies dating from the 5th or 6th century were found at nearby Spetisbury Rings in 1857. He also points out that the ancient Celtic word for river is "cale" and the old English word "burn". There is a River Cale near Sturminster Newton, "ex" means out of - put all this together and you have an explanation for Excalibur! Maybe this is just an argument for the theory that if you look hard enough you will find evidence for what you want! Whatever the truth, Badbury is certainly worth a visit.

Interestingly, some scholars have speculated that Gildas may have written his "On the Ruin and Conquest of Britain" in Dorset. His geographical

*Left: The River Cale - could this be the place where Arthur received Excalibur?*

knowledge of the south seems far better than other places he talks about and the position of Dorset, as an enclave of civilisation on the border of lands already taken over by heathens, adds weight to the argument. However, if Gildas was writing just after these events and the Battle of Mount Badon was in Dorset, why does he not mention Arthur?

Martin Henig writing in British Archaeology thinks he may have the answer. He claims the real Arthur was Ambrosius Aurelianus, an historical figure whom Gildas names as the British leader at Mount Badon. Ambrosius was reputedly from a noble Roman family, possibly even the son of an emperor. Gildas credits Ambrosius as being the inspiration and driving force behind a British renaissance. Henig explains that Ambrosius was probably known in Celtic as "Artos" meaning "the bear". It was common for late Roman soldiers to wear animal skins and "Artos" might simply have been a nickname.

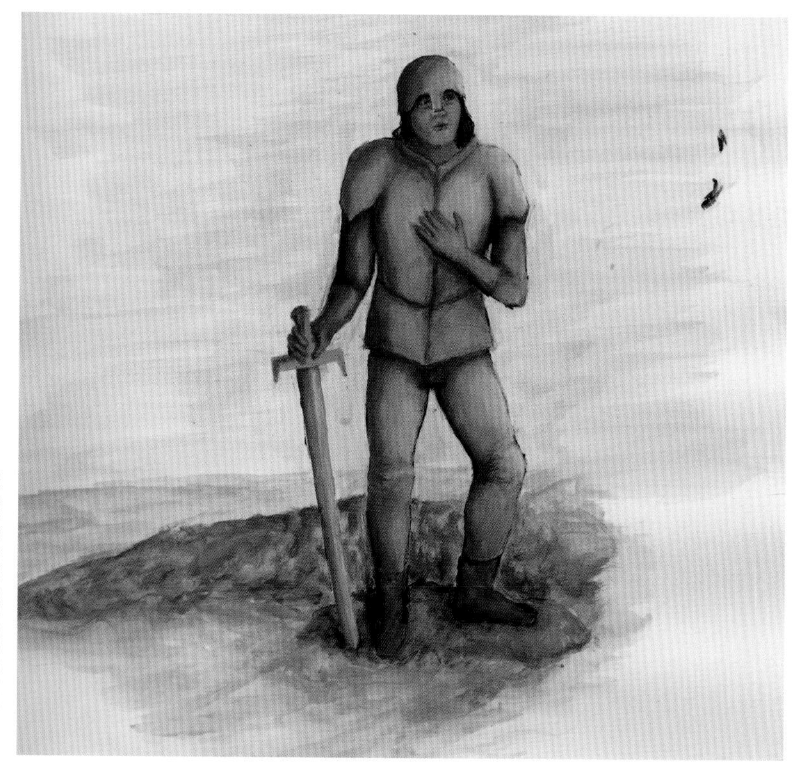



*Was there really an Arthur? Did he ever fight on Dorset soil? Perhaps Dorset had its own Dark Age hero, now forgotten; maybe a local leader who tried to rally resistance against the Saxons.*

# Saxons and Vikings

In the 540s when Gildas was writing he seems to think that the peace established by Ambrosius was threatened. During this time Saxon settlements were not far from Dorset, probably centred around Southampton Water. In AD 552 the Saxons under Cynric won a victory over the Britons at Old Sarum, and it may have been this event that precipitated an end to the brief British revival.

Little is known of the Saxon conquest of Dorset, it is simply apparent that by around AD 700 they were well established there. A victory by the Saxon leader Cenwalh at a battle in Somerset in AD 645 may have been another defining moment. Saxon burials in Dorset dating from the 7th century include women and children in what look like family groups, suggesting that Saxon settlements were already well established by that time. There is no archaeological evidence for major warfare in Dorset at this time, nor are there any written records of such. Maybe Dorset became Saxon by a gradual process of integration and assimilation, with a pragmatic population accepting the rule of their new masters and their customs.

*Above: Old Sarum castle was a Norman stronghold and site of the first cathedral whose foundations can still be seen. It was previously the scene of a crucial Saxon victory over the Britons.*

*Above: Bokerley Dyke is still an impressive earthwork and is part of a wider, ancient landscape. Just behind where the photograph was taken are two Bronze Age round barrows and nearby are the Iron Age hillfort of Penbury Knoll and the Roman road, Ackling Dyke.*

**Bokerley Dyke**

Bokerley Dyke can be best accessed from the Hampshire village of Martin, north-west of Fordingbridge. Follow the signs to Damerham and turn there towards Martin. Turn left in Martin by the small village green and there is a car park at the end of the track. [GR 058191, OS sheet 184]

You will find yourself on a beautiful remnant of chalk downland, farmed in a traditional way and famous for wild flowers and butterflies. Paths lead to a ridge topped by Bokerley Dyke which, for several miles, forms the county border between Dorset and Hampshire.

The dyke is believed to have been built in the 4th century AD as a defence against the Saxon invaders. Even today it looks an impressive obstacle, but there is still much doubt and debate over its original purpose. For some this will add to its charm and mystery; it remains a place worth visiting for the beauty and peace of its location.

*Left; The village of Worth Matravers. "Worth" is old English for "enclosure", Matravers is the name of the person it belonged to.*

The main evidence for eventual Saxon domination of Dorset comes from place names. Almost all Dorset place names are derived from old English, very few Celtic names remain. The migration of relatively small numbers of settlers would not have led to such a comprehensive change in the language, yet there is a surprising lack of archaeological evidence of Anglo-Saxons in Dorset. After all, French did not become the everyday language after the Norman Conquest. Why the British language disappeared remains a bit of a mystery. This is especially true of Wessex, since there is evidence here of co-operation between the Saxon invaders and the native Britons.

Many Dorset villages have names derived from old English because new settlements were started there by the Saxons. "Bourne", "field", "ham", "ton [or tun]", "worth" and "mere" are all from old English and by the start of the 9$^{th}$ century Dorset was probably organised into "hundreds". A hundred was the unit of land that could roughly support a hundred families, further divided into "hides", each capable of supporting one family. At the time of the Domesday survey in 1086 there were 39 such hundreds in Dorset. Thus a hundred was considerably larger than modern day parishes.

The first recorded use of the word "Dorset" comes from the Anglo-Saxon Chronicle, a record of Anglo-Saxon history begun by Alfred the Great. The name itself derives from the old English Dornsaete, meaning people who lived around Dorchester. Part of the entry for the year AD 837 says "Alderman Ethelhelm also, with the men of Dorsetshire, fought with the Danish army in Portland - isle, and for a while put them to flight; but in the end the Danes became masters of the field, and slew the ealderman." Viking raids were to become part of life for the Anglo-Saxons, particularly those on or near to the coast. The above entry in the famous chronicle tells us that Dorset was now a shire and had an ealderman with sufficient authority and organisation to gather together a local defence force.

As we have seen the Anglo-Saxons divided the land up into units known as "hides" and "hundreds". It is not certain when these divisions originated, but a society based on agriculture must introduce some method of dividing up the land for administrative purposes. The larger division of the "shire" came later when administrative districts were set up around important towns. Thus Dorset was simply the region dependent on the town of Dorchester, Hampshire the region dependent on Hamtun [Southampton].

Each hundred held meetings, usually every four weeks, where justice was dispensed for local crimes and taxes were discussed and agreed with representatives of the king. The meeting places were open air, often at the edge of the hundred and possibly at a prominent feature of the landscape. The meeting place of the hundred of Knowlton was the Neolithic henge monument where a church was subsequently built. Eggardon Hill was another ancient site used as a hundred meeting place.

*Below: The Iron Age hillfort of Eggardon Hill where a Saxon "hundred" met.*

*Above: Poole harbour viewed from Lake. A Roman port facility had been built here. It is intriguing to wonder whether the Vikings made use of any remnants of it.*

In March 978 King Edward, the son and heir to Edgar was hunting in Dorset. He decided to call in on his stepmother Aelfthryth who was staying at Corfe. He must have been on good relations with her, but before he could dismount from his horse he was stabbed and killed by members of her household. His body was thrown down a well. Historians have always thought that Aelfthryth was involved and that she wanted her son Aethelred to succeed to the throne. This is what happened; unfortunately he did not make a good king, Danish attacks got worse and Aethelred was forced to pay huge sums of money as "Danegeld"; payoffs for the Vikings to stay away.

Edward's body was recovered and taken to Wareham and later to Shaftesbury Abbey [see notes on Shaftesbury]. In the dark days that followed his death, stories of miracles grew up surrounding his body and his short reign was viewed in a rose-coloured light. The truth is that he was never a popular character, renowned in his youth for a violent temper. Had he survived he would probably not have been any better than the king schoolchildren have come to know as "Ethelred the Unready".

By the end of the tenth century Dorset was suffering more than ever from Viking raids. Viking longships had been improved and the journey from Denmark was little trouble. Portland was again ravaged in 982 and Poole harbour was used as a base in 998 from where raiding parties went all over Dorset. Nowhere was now safe. The Anglo-Saxon Chronicles for 982 tell us that three ships plundered Portland and that also in that year London was burned. Although we have come to regard the reign of Ethelred as the time when Danegeld was paid to the Vikings to keep them away, the Chronicles reveal that, in 998, several armies were put together in Dorset to try and stop them but were always defeated. The following years saw more and more Danish raids; huge sums of money were paid to buy them off. In the end they were masters of all England and in 1016 the Dane Canute was accepted as king. Although ruthless he was a strong king and brought a period of relative peace to the besieged inhabitants of Dorset. Canute liked Wessex and died in the abbey in Shaftesbury. He was buried in Winchester Cathedral where his casket can still be seen.

The story of the rest of the 11th century is fairly well known; Edward the Confessor restored the English line to the throne when Canute's died out. His reliance on help from the Normans led to the disputed succession and eventual conquest by Duke William of Normandy in 1066.

*Above: The view towards Christchurch Harbour from Hengistbury Head. Many Viking ships have sailed up these calm waters. The town visible in the distance was fortified by the Saxons under Alfred and the headland must have provided an excellent lookout.*

**Shaftesbury**

In about AD 700 the West Saxons established a settlement at Tisbury, now a small country town in Wiltshire a few miles east of Shaftesbury. After the threat from Viking armies became all too apparent, Alfred the Great recognised the defensive potential of a nearby point of land 750 feet above sea level and surrounded on three sides by steep slopes. Thus in about 880 he founded the defended town or "burgh" known as Shaftesbury. So confident was he of this new town's defences that in 888 he founded an abbey there and made his daughter the first abbess.

Shaftesbury grew in prosperity and King Athelstan authorised two mints there to strike coins. In 979 the body of the young King Edward was brought from Wareham and buried in the abbey. Shaftesbury's prosperity was assured in 1001 when Edward was canonised and Shaftesbury became a place of pilgrimage. It was reputedly a favourite place of King Canute who died there in 1035.

The Domesday survey of 1086 records Shaftesbury as having lost 80 of the 257 houses it had prior to the conquest. Nevertheless the abbey continued to grow richer until it was dissolved by Henry VIII.

Today the town is a quiet but thriving community, proud of its historic past. The abbey is now reduced to its foundations but an informative museum and pretty garden make it worth a visit. The body of King Edward the Martyr is no longer there but a shrine has been dedicated to him in the gardens. Outside the abbey is a lovely walk with spectacular views over the Vale of Blackmore.

*Above: The meagre remains of Shaftesbury Abbey.*

*Above: Corfe Castle viewed from Corfe Common showing its unique strategic position on a hilltop in the only gap in the chalk ridge.*

**Corfe Castle**

No visitor to Corfe Castle can fail to appreciate how important a position it occupies. The natural erosion of two streams has cut a gap in the Purbeck hills, leaving a steep hill in the middle. Its site is an obvious place for a castle; combine that with its position guarding a route to Poole Harbour and it is not surprising there has been an important stronghold here since Saxon times.

Corfe must have been an important fortification against raids on the Dorset coast to the south. We can imagine local villagers rushing up the hill to the safety of the timber walls as news of a raid arrived. Following the conquest the Normans recognised the strategic importance of Corfe and rebuilt the castle in stone. It was greatly enlarged and enhanced by King John and it became one of his favourite residences. Its demise following a siege by Parliamentarians in the Civil War is well known, but the remains still stand proudly and it is not difficult to imagine the scene in Saxon times with thatched huts surrounding the castle hill with its timber buildings and palisade.

*The Vikings were expert sailors. Their ships were the fastest of the time and they undertook long and perilous journeys. Harbours such as those at Poole and Christchurch were ideal bases for the Vikings to carry out raids along the rivers that radiate from them.*
*© Anthony Wootten 2006*

# Viking raids

The Viking raid has become part of English folklore. There is little doubt that for those inhabitants living close to the coast or navigable rivers at the time, the threat of such raids generated a terror that it is difficult for us to imagine. The Vikings were expert sailors and had the fastest ships of the day. They were well trained warriors with good equipment and, perhaps contrary to popular opinion, planned their attacks well.

Consider what it must have been like for small communities and monasteries near the coast. They must have been constantly on the lookout for the sight of the feared longships. The word must soon have spread that the Vikings did not just take what they wanted and leave, they came to fight and kill also.

Scholars are still not sure what drove the Vikings to expand from their homeland; it may have been population pressure on limited agricultural land. Viking beliefs help to partly explain their motives. They believed there was no life after death except for warriors, hence the drive to go and fight. They also believed that death was predetermined and that you could do nothing to alter your allotted time. It made sense therefore to go and fight and take what you could - if your time was not up you would return unhurt! Strangely the Vikings believed theft was abhorrent. To thieve would lead to an afterlife in torment. Fighting,

*Left: Wareham Quay. At the far end of Poole Harbour, Wareham provided access to the hinterland along the rivers Frome and Piddle.*

killing and then claiming booty was perfectly all right, even if the victims were innocent and defenceless.

There is an interesting story from "Egil's saga", a well known piece of Icelandic literature, which helps illustrate this mentality. Egil was a Viking who led a raid on an isolated farm. He cannot have been a formidable warrior as he was captured by the farmer and tied up along with his men. During the night they freed themselves, took what they could and left. On the way back it occurred to Egil that he had stolen the farmer's belongings. Considering this was wrong, he returned, set fire to the farm and butchered the farmer and his family as they ran out. He returned to his ship happy that he had done the honourable thing by fighting for his booty!

The number of Viking raiders in a party could vary from a handful to several hundred. As their ambitions grew and their intention graduated towards conquest, whole armies landed and established bases wherever they could find enough provisions.

As we have seen, the Anglo-Saxon Chronicles record a number of raids on Dorset. There are likely to have been others, small smash and grab raids involving one or two longships. It must have been a worrying time for the people living near the Dorset coast. Their terror was soon to be shared by those living inland as the Danish army under Guthrum began its planned conquest of the only English kingdom not under their control, Wessex.

What happened next is well documented. When all looked lost, a leader emerged who was to become the only English king for whom we use the epithet "Great". Alfred did not start well and famously hid in marshland to avoid being taken. Somehow he recovered enough fighting men to form an army, eventually defeated the Danes and established Wessex as a powerful kingdom.

After a golden age which included the reign of Edgar, Viking raids resumed with even bigger and faster ships. Dorset was once again ravaged. Whole armies of Danes roamed the land taking what they wanted and killing as they went. There is no archaeological record of Viking atrocities, but the descriptions in the Anglo-Saxon Chronicles leave no doubt that this was a very "dark age" for the people of Dorset. Presumably, however, it was not in the Vikings' interest to lay waste to the countryside they passed through. There are many records of them being bought off by payments of "Danegeld". Although they thought nothing of butchering the inhabitants, they nevertheless had to live off the land themselves for long campaigns.

**Wareham**

Wareham was one of three Dorset towns listed as a fortified burgh by a set of early documents known as the "Burghal Hidage". Christchurch was another one but has only recently been part of Dorset. These fortifications were constructed on the orders of Alfred the Great with the aim of providing a chain of defences against Viking raiders where the local population could shelter. As we have seen, Wareham was in a particularly important location where the rivers Frome and Piddle enter Poole Harbour. From their safe moorings around the vast harbour Viking longships used the rivers to venture further inland.

Fortunately the rivers could also be used as part of the town's defences, with the harbour they offered some protection on three sides of the town. Alfred probably improved the town walls that already existed. There is evidence to show that timber walls were built on the ramparts. Wareham is the only place in Dorset where the Saxon defences can still be seen. Signs in the town guide visitors on a "walls walk". As you enter Wareham from the east the Saxon earth bank can clearly be seen on the right and left of the road. Sitting on top of it on the left is the only substantially Saxon church in Dorset, St. Martin's. It is thought to have been built around 1030 and although later alterations have been made the nave is unmistakably Saxon. Today it continues to be used for worship and is well worth a visit. Inside is a famous carved effigy of Lawrence of Arabia as well as beautiful 12th century wall paintings.

*The quay at Wareham*

# St. Aldhelm

St. Aldhelm was born in Wessex in AD 639 to royal parents, possibly a nephew or cousin of King Ine. His parents may, in fact, have been among the first Anglo-Saxon converts to Christianity. Aldhelm was a prodigy; sent to school in the abbey at Canterbury, he amazed his teachers with his progress in Greek and Latin.

On returning to Wessex he joined a company of monks at Malmesbury in Wiltshire. There his reputation as a scholar grew and grew and he soon found himself leading the community. Eventually the community was formed into a regular monastery following the Benedictine rule and Aldhelm became the first abbot. As well as a scholar Aldhelm was an accomplished musician, famously preaching to the common people after gaining their attention by first busking on a busy bridge. He visited Rome and remained as Abbot of Malmesbury for thirty-three years. Many of his writings survive including an intriguing collection of riddles on many subjects.

In AD 705 Aldhelm was appointed the first Bishop of Sherborne. The Bishopric of Wessex was split in two with Winchester remaining as the other centre. A new church was built and Aldhelm continued as bishop until he died in 709.

Whilst at Sherborne, Aldhelm wrote a letter to the British kingdom of Devon and Cornwall. This is interesting as it tells us something about relationships between the newly arrived Saxons and the

*Left and above: Interior and exterior views of beautiful Sherborne Abbey on the site of the Saxon church of Aldhelm.*

*Above: St. Aldhelm's chapel near Worth Matravers*

Britons who had been forced into the western extremities of England, but still retained their independence. Remember, Dorset was then on the edge of this divide. Aldhelm's letter exhorts the British priests to conform to the Anglo-Saxon method of calculating the time of Easter and their form of the tonsure. Although he is firm in his convictions he writes with respect to the Britons and it is clear that civil relations did exist between the two kingdoms.

As well as helping establish the nunnery of St. Mary at Wareham, Aldhelm had a church built at Langton Matravers and a royal palace at Corfe. A small, windswept Norman chapel on the beautiful St. Aldhelm's Head on the Isle of Purbeck bears his name. When or by whom this was built remains something of a mystery. It is Norman in style although the present building may have replaced an earlier one. Some recent research indicates there may well have been an early Christian place of worship there.

Sherborne Abbey remains one of Dorset's finest buildings. Following the Norman Conquest it was granted full abbey status and remained as such until the dissolution of the monasteries under Henry VIII. The present church had by then only just been completed. Luckily it was not destroyed but was bought by the people of Sherborne to use as their parish church.

# Domesday Dorset

In 1066 the age of Saxon kings came to a close. Everyone knows the story of the Norman Conquest; how Duke William claimed he had been made heir by Edward the Confessor and that Harald had promised to support his claim to the throne. Less well known is the fact that William already had family connections to the West Saxon royal household. Edward the Confessor had been the son of Ethelred the Unready and his second wife Emma, sister of Richard II, Duke of Normandy. This made Edward a cousin of William's father.

Thus William's claim to be the rightful king of England was not unreasonable. Although we talk about the "conquest", William did not see it this way. He saw himself as simply and forcibly taking what was rightfully his. In the early years of his reign he sought to rule and manage the kingdom as it was. Saxons continued to hold high office and many were important members of William's administration. The revolts in the north of England and the West Country between 1068 and

*Above: Place Mill, Christchurch. There has been a mill here since Saxon times. Originally owned by the priory, the mill is mentioned in the Domesday book. Some Saxon stonework can still be seen in the outer walls.*

*Above: The ancient village of Abbotsbury. There may have been one of the earliest Christian churches in Britain here. The area was later ravaged by Saxon pirates. The abbey of St. Peter was founded by King Canute's steward, Orc.*

1071 changed all this. William put the uprisings down in a savage and ruthless manner. As a consequence the old Anglo-Saxon aristocracy was all but destroyed. Almost all were dispossessed and their lands given to Norman lords who had served the Conqueror.

Following the West Country rebellion of 1068 William marched his army through Dorset to Exeter. Some Dorset towns had allied themselves to the rebellion and as he went through William dealt with those towns in his usual brutal manner. As we shall see a little later, the destruction in the major boroughs recorded by Domesday was considerable.

In 1086 William decided he needed an accurate picture of what was going on in his kingdom. In particular he wanted to know what resources were at his disposal. The result, of course, was the most famous survey in English history, the Domesday book. Although prepared twenty years after the Battle of Hastings, the Domesday book gives a picture of life in Anglo-Saxon times. The countryside it describes with its manors, villages, churches and mills is the countryside built up by hundreds of years of Anglo-Saxon culture and administration. William did not seek to change this, merely to take full advantage of its riches.

*Above: The most complete Saxon church in Dorset, St. Martin's, Wareham sits on top of the town walls built to protect the town from Viking raiders. The church dates from around 1030 and is possibly on the site of an old Roman temple. It was one of few buildings to survive the great fire in 1762. Inside is a magnificent effigy of Lawrence of Arabia and medieval wall paintings.*

*Right: The present manor house at Cranborne is on an even more ancient site. In Saxon times Cranborne was an important abbey with a daughter house at Tewkesbury; a role that was later reversed. After the conquest Cranborne became a favourite hunting base of the Normans and a royal lodge was built here.*

It is fascinating to look at the Domesday entries for Dorset: it soon becomes clear that in some ways not much has changed. The familiar towns and villages are almost all there, as are the churches and abbeys. In some places field boundaries still follow those established in the Anglo-Saxon era. Much of the present countryside and coastline would be recognised by the people of ancient Wessex.

In many ways, of course, there have been massive changes. No large urban areas existed in the time of Domesday; the population of modern Dorset is vastly more than it was then. The huge fields of the chalk downs would be an amazing sight to ancient farmers.

So what do we know about Dorset in 1086? For a start it was owned by less than a hundred individuals or establishments. The chief landowners were the King, Norman nobles and the Church. Only a few Saxon thanes were left of the old aristocracy holding land. There were important abbeys at Cerne, Sherborne, Cranborne, Milton, Abbotsbury and Horton. Other abbeys such as Winchester also held land in Dorset, as did several in France, proof of William's determination to reward his supporters.

Four Dorset boroughs are recorded by the Domesday survey; Dorchester, Bridport, Wareham and Shaftesbury. Looking at the entries for these in Domesday gives some indication of the hardships suffered by the population in the years after 1066. In Dorchester in 1066 it says there were 172 houses and that they paid tax to the King for 10 hides. A hide was roughly the unit of land sufficient to support a family. There has been much debate as to how big it might have been, there seems to have been no fixed measurement. It may have been as much as 120 acres, but probably less, say 30 to 50 acres. Pasture was not included, a hide was land under the plough. In 1086 the survey records only 88 houses with 100 having been completely destroyed. No explanation is given for the arithmetic!

A similar picture emerges for Wareham. There were 143 houses in 1066; by 1086 there were only 70 with 73 having been completely destroyed. They too paid tax on 10 hides. Shaftesbury, as we have seen before, was an important Saxon centre with its hill top position and powerful abbey. Domesday records 66 houses there with 38 having been destroyed. Interestingly, it says that in the part belonging to the abbess there were 153 houses before 1066, with 111 left and 42 "utterly destroyed". It records there having been 3 mints in the town. In Bridport before 1066 there were 120 houses but only 5 hides. Domesday records 100 houses with 20 so badly neglected that those who lived in them were not able to pay tax. Were these people refugees who had occupied derelict properties or perhaps the original occupants who had fallen on hard times since the conquest?

Wimborne is not recorded as a borough by Domesday but it is obvious nevertheless that it was an important place. We are told that King Edward held Wimborne, Shapwick, Moor Crichel and Wimborne St. Giles. There is no record of the number of hides because before 1066 they did not pay tax. However, we are told that there was land for 45 ploughs and that no fewer than 8 mills served the population. All in all it seems to have been a thriving community.

## Christchurch and Hengistbury Head

Hengistbury Head lies to the south of Christchurch Harbour and commands sweeping views in all directions. There is a large car park at GR 162910, OS map 195. Many paths lead over and around the headland. It is an intriguing place with a fascinating history. Archaeology tells us that Hengistbury was an important Neolithic and Bronze Age site but really came into its own during the Iron Age when it was a centre for the embryonic iron industry. Local ore from the cliffs in the form of ironstone nodules or "doggers" were smelted on site. This activity continued into the Roman times but when the legions left Hengistbury seems to have returned to wilderness. Perhaps here is one example of how the infrastructure collapsed at the end of Roman rule.

Hengistbury is named after Hengist, brother of Horsa, leaders of the first Saxons in these islands whom Vortigern famously invited as mercenaries. However, it is unclear what the headland has to do with Hengist as he almost certainly did not come ashore here. Christchurch was fortified by Alfred in the fight against Viking raiders and Hengistbury may well have been an important look out.

Walk up onto the headland and admire the wonderful views over Christchurch and its harbour. The defended Saxon town was where the town centre now is, in between the rivers Stour and Avon as they flow into the harbour. It is easy to see how this would have provided an attractive haven for Viking longships.

*Left: Steep Gold Hill, Shaftesbury shows why the site was chosen by the Saxons for a defended burgh. Below: Christchurch Harbour - a magnet for Vikings.*

**Milton Abbey**

Milton Abbey and its neighbouring village Milton Abbas form one of the most picturesque and enchanting corners of Dorset. Now attached to a famous public school, the abbey was founded in AD 933 by King Athelstan in memory of his brother Edwin who was tragically killed at sea. Some historians believe Athelstan was responsible for his brother's death, a result of unfounded rumours of treachery started by jealous rivals, and that the king built the abbey to atone for his sin. The abbey was bestowed with numerous manors in Dorset totalling about 67 hides. Athelstan also buried his mother here and arranged for the procurement of many religious relics including the bones of St. Sampson and the arm of St. Branwalader.

In 964 the priests of Milton were replaced by monks from Glastonbury under reforms carried out by King Edgar and Archbishop Dunstan. Milton Abbey then continued as a Benedictine house for over five hundred years until the dissolution of the monasteries by Henry VIII, who gave the abbey and its estate to Sir John Tregonwell. The present church was begun after the previous one had been struck by lightning in 1309. It was never properly completed and reached its current stage at the turn of the 15th century.

The present school was the house of Joseph Damer who bought the estate in 1752. He soon became Baron Milton and enlisted Capability Brown to design the grounds. Although a flourishing school, visitors are welcomed to the abbey and the grounds. When the first XI are playing cricket in the summer there is no finer visual representation of England - Athelstan, her first king, would have been proud!

The Domesday book itself is a dry volume, merely listing hides, ploughs, mills, slaves and so on. What is interesting is to visit some of Dorset's ancient villages and consider how, in some ways, little has changed since the monumental survey was undertaken. I have chosen a few such places in various parts of the county; all have remained agricultural communities since Saxon times and are well worth a visit for those wanting to discover some of old England.

**Ashmore** in north Dorset near the border with Wiltshire is one of the highest villages in Dorset. It has a pond in the centre of the village that apparently dates from Roman times and, somewhat unusually given its height, hardly ever dries up. In 1086 Ashmore paid tax for 8 hides, of which 4 were held by the lord. There were 10 villagers, 6 smallholders and 8 slaves. Today cottages cluster around the pond much as they must have done in Saxon times. The small church is close by and the village is still surrounded by fields divided by hedgerows.

**Cranborne** is today a thriving village centred around a square on the edge of Cranborne Chase. It has two pubs, a restaurant and the well known "Ancient Technology Centre". It also has one of the most beautiful manor houses in England, begun in the time of Henry VIII, but on the site of a much older establishment. Domesday records Cranborne as a thriving village with 10 hides and 4 mills. Three thanes still held land there. Cranborne was also the site of an important abbey, founded around 980 by a Saxon nobleman named Haylward Snew. By all accounts he was a very handsome young man; he seems to have married happily and when he died was buried in the abbey he had founded. His grandson Brihtric, who enlarged the abbey, was involved in affairs of state and found himself on a diplomatic mission to Normandy. While there he met a certain lady named Matilda. Brihtric may well have inherited some of his grandfather's appeal because it seems Matilda offered him her hand in marriage. When spurned by Brihtric she turned instead to Duke William and subsequently became his wife. Poor Brihtric cannot possibly have imagined what a mistake this would turn out to be. Matilda did not forget her rejection and after the conquest persuaded William to seize Cranborne Abbey and Brihtric. He was thrown into prison in Winchester where he died.

*The ancient pond at Ashmore.*

One of the most atmospheric places in Dorset, **Tyneham** is a perfect illustration of how rural life went on, virtually unchanged, for centuries before the industrial revolution and the huge population growth of the modern age. The story of Tyneham is well known in Dorset. Now a derelict and abandoned village, its inhabitants were evicted by the military in 1943 so that their land could be used for preparations in the build up to D-Day. It was, perhaps, a small sacrifice compared to some that were made, but it must have been heartbreaking at the time. At least the army has preserved the peace and tranquility of the village and it makes for a great day out. Tyneham is on the coast between Lulworth Cove and Kimmeridge. There is a small minor road that leads up the chalk escarpment from the village of East Lulworth and it is signposted from that. The road is in the army ranges and not always open. It is, however, always open during school holidays and most weekends. Check on www.lulworth.com/ranges.htm or ring 01929 462721 ext. 4819. In late Saxon times Tyneham had 3½ hides with 3 villagers and 4 smallholders. There was a mere 2 acres of meadow. Looking at the ruined village now we can see that it wasn't much bigger a millenium later. The lines of cottages between the pond and the church probably formed the pattern for the village throughout the centuries. It is a short walk down a track to Worbarrow Bay, a charming beach where, like at Lulworth, the sea has eroded the softer strata between the Purbeck and Portland limestones and the Chalk. At the entrance to a smaller cove on the southern side are massive concrete blocks, erected

in the war years as defence against a possible German invasion. It is intriguing to wonder what, if any, defences were built at the same spot to deter Viking raiders a thousand years before.

**Kimmeridge** must have been another settlement where the inhabitants lived in fear of Viking raids, although the hard rock ledges stretching out to sea may not have been the easiest things to land longships on. In Roman times Kimmeridge had been important as a centre for craftsmen working the hard shale into ornaments and jewellery. No mention is made of this in Domesday which records only 2 villagers and 8 smallholders. There were, however, 2 cows, 16 pigs, 250 sheep and 1 horse. As with Tyneham, Kimmeridge remained a small agricultural village for hundreds of years. Unlike Tyneham it has survived into the modern era and although tourism is now a vital factor in the local economy, agriculture remains important. Back in 1086 Kimmeridge was part of the estate of the abbey at Cerne Abbas. Today, much of the village and surrounding area is still the property of a large landowner, the Smedmore estate; hence the toll motorists must pay to drive to the large car park on the cliff top.

*Above left: A medieval painting in Milton Abbey church of King Athelstan.*
*Below left: The entrance to the present church at Milton Abbey on the site of the abbey founded by King Athelstan.*

*Below: The small harbour in Kimmeridge Bay. A small agricultural community in Saxon times, Kimmeridge once had a thriving jewellery industry.*

**Cerne Abbas**

If any place conjures up an atmosphere of ancient mysteries it is Cerne Abbas, tucked in hidden green valleys at the foot of the chalk uplands. Debate still rages as to whether the famous giant, carved into the chalk hillside at the entrance to the village, is an ancient work of art celebrating the god Hercules or a huge, ridiculing caricature of Oliver Cromwell.

Although it is the giant that attracts the visitors there are hidden gems in this village that will delight discerning tourists. A Benedictine abbey was founded here in 987 but legend associates an earlier one with St. Augustine. The story says he was at first treated rudely by locals here, but prophesied that they would repent and turn to God. He was right and gave the place the name "Cernel", a combination of the Latin word cerno, meaning "I perceive" and the Hebrew word El meaning "God". He is said to have struck the ground with his staff whereupon a spring gushed forth. The abbey had a long, prosperous and peaceful history. There is not much to be seen today but what remains is in an utterly idyllic setting. The Abbot's Porch and the Guest House or Hospice are in the grounds of the privately owned Abbey House, but entry is usually allowed for a nominal fee.

Nearby, in the corner of a graveyard, is St. Augustine's Well. Another twist of the St. Augustine legend says that he asked local shepherds if they would prefer beer or water to drink. Impressed by their temperate reply of water, he then struck the ground with his staff. It is thought the whole St. Augustine story was made up by scheming monks to attract more pilgrims, but there is another story attached to the well which is more likely to be true. Edwold, son of Edmund, king of the East Anglians, sought the life of a hermit after his brother had been killed by the Danes. He had a vision of a silver well and found it at Cerne Abbas where he lived until he died. He was later canonised and the well is also known as the Silver Well. It is still a peaceful and atmospheric spot.

*Opposite page: The Silver Well in Cerne Abbas.*
*Top: The Guest House or Abbot's Hospice - once part of Cerne Abbey.*
*Bottom left: The Abbot's Porch at Cerne Abbey.*
*Bottom right: Detail of the Abbot's Porch.*

**Bibliography and further reading:**

Saxons and Vikings - David A. Hinton [Dovecote Press]

Domesday Book, Dorset [Phillimore]

In Search of the Dark Ages - Michael Wood [BBC]

Alfred Warrior King - John Peddle [Sutton Publishing]

The Anglo-Saxon World - Sir Frank Stenton [Oxford Universtiy Press]

Proceedings of the Dorset Natural History and Archaeological Society
"The Welsh in Dorset" - Thomas Kerslake [Vol. 3]
"Normans in Dorset" - CWH Dicker [Vol. 31]
"Badbury Rings Reviewed" - EC Chancellor [Vol. 66]

Useful and interesting web sites:

www.britannia.com - excellent summaries of key episodes and you can also find complete texts such as the "Anglo-Saxon Chronicles"
www.earlybritishkingdoms.com - very comprehensive site
www.lib.rochester.edu/CAMELOT/arthmenu.htm - American university site on Arthur
www.fordham.edu/halsall/sbook.htm - includes a "medieval source book" - huge amount of information
www.localhistories.org/saxon.htm - a comprehensive section on "Anglo-Saxon and Viking England" by Tim Lambert
www.historymedren.about.com - another huge site, you can find the whole of Nennius' "History of Britain" here.